MAGIC MOUNTAIN®

An Environmental Children's Program

CURRICULUM GUIDE

Including Basic, Art, Music, and Outdoor Education Curriculum

Ages: 4 – 11
Grades: Pre – K through 5th

Lisa Dancing-Light, BME, Educational Specialist

©2021 Dancing Light Enterprises, LLC

Published by
Dancing Light Enterprises, LLC
Carbondale, Colorado

ISBN: 978-1-7365012-4-5

lisadancinglight.com

Light of the Moon, Inc.
Partnering with self-published authors since 2009
Book Design/Production/Consulting
Carbondale, Colorado • www.lightofthemooninc.com

WELCOME TO PARENTS AND TEACHERS!

Thank you for choosing Magic Mountain Curriculum Guide. This eight-week syllabus is foundational to the complete Environmental Children's Program, custom designed for diverse learning styles to integrate fresh resources to your existing program. Before you begin your journey be sure you have several copies of A SONG AND STORY OF MAGIC MOUNTAIN® in English and Spanish or request them from your local library. Magic Mountain Songs CD is available at lisadancinglight.com or stream on YouTube.

Magic Mountain Basic Curriculum will support students:
- to grow self-confidence and awareness
- to stimulate and nurture curiosity and creativity
- to inspire and explore the wonders of nature
- to develop greater sensitivity and stronger critical thinking skill sets

This program synthesizes more than forty years of my educational expertise, professional trainings and personal experiences. You now have a field-tested program to add to your existing curriculum. Some terms included here may be familiar and some may be new. For example, *Brain Gym*® exercises are part of the Whole Brain Integration Edu-K program, developed by Dr. Paul Dennison. His work partnered perfectly with my mentorship and study with Don Campbell, author of *Introduction to the Musical Brain* as well as my advanced trainings with Educational Psychologist, Dr. Mary Meeker, developer of SOI, proving intellectual abilities. My study of T'ai Chi, Qi Gong and my certification as a yoga instructor all support the Brain-Body connection. Decades of classical training in piano and certifications in the Suzuki Method, along with my study with several neurologists all confirm how important music and movement are for the brain. Most of all, my love of performing and songwriting are woven sweetly into the music segment, which can culminate in the performance of Magic Mountain® – The Musical.

I hope this valuable tool cultivates rich experiences exploring art, music and nature's beauty in your home, and in your classroom. I look forward to seeing your photos and hearing about your experiences as you share your journey on our Facebook: MagicMountainBook or my website: lisadancinglight.com.

May this journey deepen your connection to nature, filling your classroom with magic!

Lisa Dancing-Light

Lisa teaching Sacred Ground at Lydia's Pre-school

MAGIC MOUNTAIN CURRICULUM GUIDE
Table of Contents

MAGIC MOUNTAIN®

An Environmental Children's Program

BASIC CURRICULUM GUIDE

Ages: 4 – 11
Grades: Pre – K through 5th

Lisa Dancing-Light, BME, Educational Specialist
Educational Consultant – Grace M. Zanni

BASIC CURRICULUM GUIDE

1. **GOAL**

2. **INTRODUCTION**

3. **OBJECTIVES**

4. **CONTENT**

5. **PROCEDURE**

6. **SKILLS**

7. **ESSENTIAL QUESTION**

8. **INTERDISCIPLINARY ACTIVITIES**
   - A. MATH
   - B. SCIENCE
   - C. MUSIC
   - D. ART
   - E. GEOGRAPHY
   - F. READING
   - G. DRAMA
   - H. MOVEMENT AND BRAIN INTEGRATION
   - I. IMAGINATION AND PLAY
   - J. LANGUAGE
   - K. WRITING
   - L. WILDLIFE

9. **RESOURCES**
   - A. SUGGESTED READING FOR CHILDREN
   - B. SUGGESTED READING FOR PARENTS AND TEACHERS

10. **STUDENT ASSESSMENT**

1. GOAL

Our goal with the Magic Mountain curriculum is to combine the freedom, curiosity, and imagination of early childhood education that takes place in forests and nature while interweaving scientific, mathematical, artistic, and musical themes.

2. INTRODUCTION

A Song and Story of Magic Mountain is about a talking mountain who goes to sleep because people stop coming to hear his stories. When two children come to camp with their parents in the valley of Magic Mountain, they learn about Magic from a wise old owl and decide to journey up the mountain to see if they can awaken him and hear his stories.

This story is an adventure into a special way of listening, of waking up, and of the beauty of nature in a changing world.

The author is also a musician and recording artist and has composed songs to accompany the story to potentially complement and enrich the eight-week study curriculum. The intention is to perform the story as a musical play for elementary grades. This story will appeal to students of all ages and suggested activities may be adapted for different age groups. Themes include the wisdom of storytelling and environmental and wildlife changes while combining elements of imagination and realism.

3. OBJECTIVES

- To listen to and enjoy a story about a very special and magical mountain
- To encourage active listening and participation in all activities
- To introduce story elements of the passage of time and changes that occur
- To learn about the components of story structure: the beginning, the middle, and the end
- To write and share original stories from the child's perspective
- To listen and to learn the original songs related to the story
- To create artistic projects relating to the story
- To celebrate and deepen a connection with nature through education and music
- To cultivate awareness of preserving and protecting our environment
- To develop sensitivity to our growing relationship with wildlife
- To develop skills for being in nature
- To gain confidence and a sense of comfort being in nature through camping and exploring
- To initiate awareness of natural forest ecosystems and botanicals

4. CONTENT
- To understand concepts and elements of imagination
- To learn about legendary stories and Indigenous peoples
- To compare and contrast the character traits of life: the mountain, the early settlers, the children, the animals, the owl, the forest, the river, and the Ouzel
- To develop an understanding of a changing landscape, cause and effect

5. PROCEDURE
- Children can tap into prior knowledge of mountains, Indigenous peoples, camping activities, and imagination
- Introduce the book, the title page, the author, and the theme song
- Children can learn about personification, how an author makes an inanimate object like a mountain, seem like a person
- Children can read the story with great expression and a sense of wonder
- After reading, children can share their favorite part or favorite character in the story
- Discuss new vocabulary words
- Close reading time by listening to one of the songs and enjoy a snack

6. SKILLS
- Listening Comprehension
- Oral language development
- Understanding personification
- Character development
- Plot structure
- Integrate neurological development

7. ESSENTIAL QUESTIONS
- Who do you think the early listeners were? What clues helped you decide?
- How did the mountain feel during the beginning, middle, and end of the story?
- What words could you use to describe the characters?
- How can you become a better listener?

8. INTERDISCIPLINARY ACTIVITIES
A. MATH

Research and compare the heights of different mountains

Use graph paper to illustrate the heights of mountains drawn to scale

Decide/guess when the mountain was born and calculate its age today

Calculate the number of steps to walk up a mountain, or on a hike

What is the tallest mountain in your state? In North America? In the world?

B. SCIENCE

Research different types of mountains and their composition

Identify indicators and effects of global warming on the alpine environment

Learn about birds, animals, plants, and trees living in an alpine environment

Observe elements of a changing landscape and give examples

C. MUSIC

Listen to, and sing along with the original songs related to the story

Write another verse for the Magic Mountain song

Sing one of the songs with another classmate

Pick a character to act out while the story is read

Make rhythm instruments

D. ART

Draw your own picture of Magic Mountain

Draw pictures of Magic Mountain in different seasons

Make clay models of the mountain at different times in the story

Design a 3-part mural showing the changes the mountain went through

Dye sheets to make costumes for the Magic Mountain or Indigenous peoples

Draw pictures of an alpine environment, with birds, lakes, vegetation

Draw pictures of things you would take hiking or camping

Make a Fairy House and create a nature environment with found objects:
    Search for How to Make a Fairy House

Make a diorama of Magic Mountain or your favorite scene in the book:
    Search for How to Make a Diorama

E. GEOGRAPHY

Introduce basic map reading skills

What is a topo map?

Bring a map and show a hiking trail up a mountain

Have children draw their own simple map

Locate the tallest mountain in Colorado, in North America, and the world

F. READING

Reread the story

Record your voice as you read the story to a partner using Soundtrap
    Search soundtrap.com

Introduce Brain Gym exercises – Do Brain Gym exercises for vision and hearing
    Watch lisadancinglight.com/tutorial

Re-record your voice and notice any differences

Group read a favorite page
Read other books, legendary stories, or poems about mountain experiences
    See resources

G. DRAMA

In pairs, act out your favorite part of the story
Pretend to be the Magic Mountain at different times in the story
Write or create a skit having children meet Magic Mountain for the first time
Group acts as special people listening to a story told by the mountain

H. MOVEMENT AND BRAIN INTEGRATION

Brain Gym Exercises: Watch lisadancinglight.com/tutorial

Brain Buttons

Place your right hand at the top of your sternum between your clavicle and first rib. Press and gently massage. This is K27 in acupuncture for the kidney meridian. Change hands and repeat. This charges the brain and the body with energy.

Thinking Caps

Place your finger on your ear flaps and unroll the skin from top to bottom three times. This activates your hearing as well as stimulates hundreds of pressure points in the body.

The Owl

Place your right hand on your left trapezius muscle and turn your head away from your hand. Scan the room visually for information, like an owl. Add an owl sound, "Who," slowly turning your head from right to left. Change hands and repeat. This allows you to hear the sound of your own voice.

Cross Crawls

Lift your right knee and tap with your left hand.

Repeat with the left hand on the right knee.

For beginners – an easy way to introduce this is by swinging your arms around your body core. Relax. This helps integrate the right and left hemispheres of your brain.

Cook's Hook Up

Stand with arms extended in front, palms facing each other, and rotate your palms out. Cross your right hand over the left and clasp your hands together. Bring your hands in toward the heart or the chest. Standing, cross one foot over the other (this can be done seated also). This posture helps calm the energy systems in the body and is especially beneficial for anxiety.

Qigong:

Shake the Tree

With feet hips width apart, feet flat on the ground, begin to bend your knees and gently bounce your body up and down. Arms are loose, shoulders soft and relaxed (1 minute).

Watch lisadancinglight.com/tutorial

Swinging and Drumming

Watch lisadancinglight.com/tutorial

Energizing the body

Pat the outside of the legs DOWN to the ankles and UP the inside of the legs. Do this three times to activate several meridians of the body.

Lymph Stimulation

Pat under your right armpit and DOWN the side body and UP the front body, pausing on the chest to tap the thymus gland. Pat down the inside of your arm to your hand and up the back side of your arm. Do this three times and repeat with the left side.

Yoga:

Mountain Pose (Tadasana)

Stand with your feet hip-width apart. Feel the four corners of the foot anchored on the floor. Lift your toes. Lower toes. Draw the head of the femur back. Draw the tailbone down. Hands at your side, palms open facing forward. Feel the chest open as well as the shoulders.

Watch lisadancinglight.com/tutorial

Standing Tree Pose (Vriksasana)

Stand with your feet hip-width apart. Arms out 45 degrees. Bring your left heel to touch your right ankle and balance. Feel the four corners of the right foot anchored on the floor. Lift the chest or heart area and breathe. Repeat with your right heel on your left ankle. Repeat the same pose with your right foot standing and your left foot raised to your upper inner thigh. Watch lisadancinglight.com/tutorial

I. IMAGINATION AND PLAY

Make a tent and pretend to go camping

Pretend to build a fire

What food would you cook for dinner?

What do you do if you have to go to the bathroom?

How would you store your food to keep it away from animals?

Bring a photo if classmates have gone on a camping trip

Have the group make up a story based on a photo

J. LANGUAGE

Vocabulary development: legend, alpine, camping words

Retell a favorite part of the story

Create relevant vocabulary lists: camping words, mountain words

Using different voices, speak like the mountain or the boy and girl

K. WRITING

Make or use journals to record daily experiences and progress

L. WILDLIFE

Become a tracker and identify tracks of different animals

Create an area with sand to identify animal tracks outside

Develop research skills

Use for science and math activities

Animal Tracking

    Search: Personal Creations Animal Tracks: How to Find Animal Tracks with Your Kids

    Always be cautious – Never feed wildlife. Attempting to pet or feed wildlife can be very dangerous

    Leave No Trace - You are a guest in nature, pack out what you carry in

    Respect the wildlife – Give animals their space

    Make loud noise and appear very big if you see a Mountain Lion or a Bear

    Tracking footprints:

        Snow: Perfect for tracking winter animals

        Mud: Animals living near water, a lake or river

        Sand: Excellent for identifying animals close to a river or water source

        Dirt: Provides great pad for footprints or larger animals

    Animal Classifications:

        Canines

        Felines

        Small Mammals

        Hooved Animals

Other ways to track besides paw prints:

    Broken branches

    Fur on branches

    Claw marks and scratches on trees

    Scat or droppings

Things You Will Need to Bring with You:

    Your Journal

    Pen or pencil

Colored pencils for drawing
Camera
Water bottle
Small backpack
Jacket or vest with good pockets
Hat
Good walking shoes

9. RESOURCES

A. SUGGESTED READING FOR CHILDREN

A Child's Introduction to the Environment – Michael Driscoll

Amelia Bedelia Goes Camping – Peggy Parish

As the Crow Flies: A First Book of Maps – Gail Hartman

A Song and Story of Magic Mountain – Lisa Dancing-Light

The Call of the Wild – Jack London

Camping Spree With Mr. Magee – Chris Van Dusen

Finding Wild – Megan Wagner Lloyd

Follow That Map! A First Book of Mapping Skills – Scot Ritchie

Fred & Ted Go Camping – Peter Anthony Eastman

Geography From A to Z: A Picture Glossary – Jack Knowlton

Goodnight, Campsite – Loretta Sponsle

I Worship Every Bird that I See – Drew Lanham

National Parks of the USA – Kate Siber

Our Great Big Backyard –Laura Bush & Jenna Bush Hager

Pocket Guide to the Outdoors – My side of the Mountain – Jean Craighead George

S Is For S'Mores – Helen Foster James

The Camping Trip – Jennifer K. Mann

The Hike – Alison Farrell

The Last Wild Witch – Starhawk

The Lorax – Dr. Seuss

The Midnight Fox – Betsy Byars

The Street Beneath My Feet – Charlotte Guillain

The Story of Jumping Mouse – John Steptoe

We Are Water Protectors – Carole Lindstrom

When We Go Camping – Margriet Ruurs

White Fang – Jack London

B. SUGGESTED READING FOR PARENTS AND TEACHERS

Behaving As If All Life Mattered – Machaelle Small Wright

Black Elk Speaks – John G. Neihardt

Braiding Sweetgrass – Robin Wall Kimmerer

Bringing the Forest School Approach to your Early Years Practice – Karen Constable

Buffalo Woman Comes Singing – Brooke Medicine Eagle

Can You Hear the Trees Talking? – Peter Wohlleben

Desert Solitaire – Edward Abbey

Finding the Mother Tree: Discovering the Wisdom of the Forest – Suzanne Simard

Fifty Places To Camp Before You Die – Chris Santella

Hike It Baby – *100 Awesome Outdoor Adventures with Babies and Toddlers* –
    Shanti Hodges

Kinship With all Life – J. Allen Boone

Like a Tree: How Trees, Women, and Tree People Can Save the Planet –
    Jean Shinoda Bolen

Many Winters – Nancy Wood

Pieces of White Shell – Terry Tempest Williams

The Hidden Life of Trees: What They Feel, How They Communicate –
    Discoveries from a Secret World – Peter Wohlleben

The Last Child in the Woods – Richard Louv

The Nature Fix: Why Nature Makes Us Happier, Healthier, and More Creative –
    Florence Williams

The Secret Life of Trees: How they Live and Why they Matter – Colin Tudge

The Secret Network of Nature: The Delicate Balance of All Living Things –
    Peter Wohlleben

The Overstory – Richard Powers

Play The Forest School Way: Woodland Games and Crafts for Adventurous Kids –
    Jane Worroll and Peter Houghton

Touch The Earth: A Self-portrait of Indian Existence – T. C. McLuhan

Our Wild Calling – Richard Louv

Walden (Life In the Woods) – Henry David Thoreau

Wild At Heart: America's Turbulent Relationship with Nature, from Exploitation to
    Redemption – Alice Outwater

10. STUDENT ASSESSMENT

Have students draw before and after pictures to depict the mountain's
    changing landscape

Ask students to tell you one or two facts they have learned by listening to
    the story and its songs

MAGIC MOUNTAIN®

An Environmental Children's Program

ART CURRICULUM GUIDE

Ages: 4 – 11
Grades: Pre – K through 5th

Lisa Dancing-Light, BME, Educational Specialist

©2021 Dancing Light Enterprises, LLC

ART CURRICULUM GUIDE

WEEK 1
RHYTHM INSTRUMENTS
JOURNALS
EARTHWATCH AREAS

WEEK 2
JOURNALS
RATTLES
MASKS

WEEK 3
MAGIC MOUNTAIN MODEL
BIRD HOUSES AND BIRD FEEDERS
DIORAMAS

WEEK 4
JOURNAL
MODEL CONSTRUCTION
COSTUMES
STAGE SETS AND PROPS

WEEK 5
JOURNAL
COSTUMES
PROP DESIGN

WEEK 6
COMPLETE DIORAMAS
EARTHWATCH AREAS

WEEK 7
COMPLETE CONSTRUCTION
COMPLETE COSTUMES
COMPLETE PROPS

WEEK 8
PERFORMANCE & VIDEO

POST PRODUCTION

WEEK 1 PLANNING NOTES

Art supplies you will need:

- ❏ Container for drums, small cardboard boxes, tin cans, plastic container with lid
- ❏ Colored paper
- ❏ Pencils, crayons, markers
- ❏ Beads
- ❏ Feathers
- ❏ Paint
- ❏ Stickers
- ❏ Journal paper

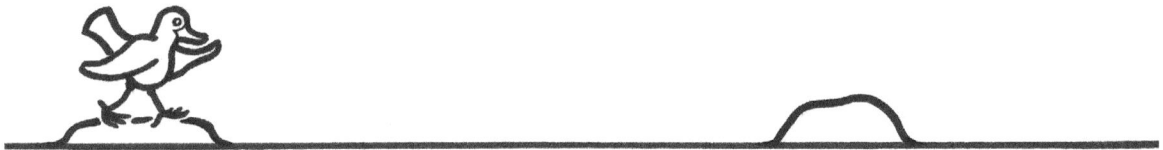

Let the journey begin!

WEEK 1
RHYTHM INSTRUMENTS – JOURNALS – EARTHWATCH AREAS

RHYTHM INSTRUMENTS – DRUMS
Make drums out of metal, cardboard, plastic, cans, or other containers
Cover with colored paper, paint, or stickers
Decorate with beads, feathers, or found objects

JOURNALS
Make a book or journal to draw and document events during each class

EARTHWATCH AREAS
Create several Earthwatch areas around your school or home to notice changes
Take a picture or draw a picture showing what is in your area
Bring samples and specimens from that space to class for your journal:

Leaves
Flowers
Grass
Pine needles
Branches
Rocks

WEEK 2 PLANNING NOTES

Art supplies you will need:

- ❏ Activa Paper Mache Mix – Non-toxic, gluten-free, 100 wheat-free, non-carcinogenic
- ❏ Elmer's Paper Mache Art Paste
- ❏ Newspaper
- ❏ Vaseline
- ❏ Small balloons for paper mache rattles
- ❏ Small, clean, empty plastic bottles, paper tubes from TP, and paper towels
- ❏ Paintbrushes
- ❏ Emulsion paint
- ❏ Corn, bean, rice
- ❏ Craft Sticks
- ❏ Feather, beads, yarn
- ❏ Table and table covering for workspace
- ❏ Felt – Black, brown, grey, yellow, white
- ❏ Elastic
- ❏ Needle & thread
- ❏ Glue gun or fabric glue
- ❏ Journal
- ❏ Drawing paper

WEEK 2
JOURNALS – RATTLES – MASKS

JOURNALS
Draw what Magic Mountain looks like
Draw trees that might grow on Magic Mountain
Draw an animal that would roam on Magic Mountain
Draw a bird that might fly around Magic Mountain

RHYTHM INSTRUMENTS – RATTLES
Make rattles with small plastic bottles, vitamin bottles, TP cardboard rolls,
or paper towel cardboard
Alternate activity: make paper mache rattles out of lightbulbs or balloons
Sticks for handles
Fill with beans, corn, rice, or small stones
Decorate rattles with feathers, beads, yarn, and paint designs

ANIMAL MASKS
Using a template, create fox, raccoon, deer, and owl masks
Use colored felt and glue layers together
Sew elastic for a custom fit

WEEK 3 PLANNING NOTES

Art supplies you will need:

- ❏ Activa Paper Mache Mix
- ❏ Elmer's Paper Mache Art Paste
- ❏ Plastic bottles
- ❏ Small wood lengths
- ❏ Saw
- ❏ Hammer
- ❏ Nails
- ❏ Wood glue
- ❏ Craft sticks
- ❏ Pine cones
- ❏ Peanut butter
- ❏ Birdseed
- ❏ Yarn for hanging pine cones
- ❏ Diorama box
- ❏ Colored paper for shapes
- ❏ Small figures for the diorama
- ❏ Found objects for the diorama

WEEK 3
MAGIC MOUNTAIN MODEL – BIRD HOUSES AND BIRD FEEDERS
– DIORAMAS

MODEL OF MAGIC MOUNTAIN
Begin construction of the Magic Mountain model with paper mache or other resources

Paint a backdrop mural or use paper, fabric, or a model for the sky – whatever is appropriate for your home, classroom, or school depending on stage size and available space. Remember: Magic talks!

BIRD HOUSES AND BIRD FEEDERS
Make bird houses or feeders out of plastic bottles or wood scraps

Cover pine cones with peanut butter mixed with birdseed to hang in a place to observe the birds feeding

DIORAMAS
Plan and assemble diorama materials to create your imaginary Magic Mountain scene

What season is your diorama?

What is growing in your diorama?

What animals would be living in your diorama?

WEEK 4 PLANNING NOTES

Art supplies you will need:

- ❑ Large sheets of white paper for the mural
- ❑ Tape to piece mural together
- ❑ Paint
- ❑ Logs
- ❑ Benches
- ❑ Journals
- ❑ Crayons, pencils, markers
- ❑ Scissors
- ❑ Colored paper for flowers
- ❑ Light brown fabric for vests
- ❑ Paper for felt or headbands
- ❑ Feather for headbands

You're halfway there!

WEEK 4
JOURNAL – MODEL CONSTRUCTION – COSTUMES – STAGE SETS AND
PROPS

JOURNAL
In your journal, draw a scene of an environmental change from the book:
The river
The Mountain
The birds
Draw scenes of environmental and seasonal changes where you live

MODEL CONSTRUCTION OF MAGIC MOUNTAIN
Continue construction of the model of Magic Mountain

COSTUMES
Begin drawing costume designs
Boy
Girl
Mother
Father
Owl
Ouzel
Indigenous storyteller
Settlers

STAGE SETS
Draw ideas for the stage area and staging for the play
Decide how many sets are appropriate for you to make
Assemble construction materials for sets
Here are some suggestions and remember to keep it simple:
Magic Mountain main set
A large cardboard or plywood model of Magic with holes for the face and arms
Logs or benches for the children to sit on
Paper flowers set in tin cans or flower pots
Christmas trees w/o lights for forest
Blue tarp for the sky background
White cardboard clouds for the tarp
Mural of the mountain range
Nature scene with animals
Nature scene with trash and a polluted river

Campfire scene with a covered wagon
Mountain-climbing scene
Camping scene – tents

PROP IDEAS
Mural for backdrop
Blue fabric or tarp for the sky
Logs or benches to sit on
Firepit or lantern
Flowers in pots
Forest trees

How's it going?

WEEK 5 PLANNING NOTES

Supplies you will need:

- ❏ Hiking clothes
- ❏ Hiking shoes
- ❏ Jacket
- ❏ Hats
- ❏ Sunglasses
- ❏ Backpacks
- ❏ Tent or tents
- ❏ Flashlights
- ❏ Owl mask or costume
- ❏ Ouzel mask or costume
- ❏ Indigenous costume
- ❏ Bandana
- ❏ Jeans
- ❏ Plaid shirts
- ❏ Black shirts and pants with no logos (optional for animal masks w/o costumes)
- ❏ Large paper sheets for the storybook model
- ❏ Easel to hold the storybook
- ❏ Rocking chair for the narrator
- ❏ Lamp
- ❏ Long dresses
- ❏ Bonnets
- ❏ Beard

WEEK 5
JOURNAL – COSTUMES – PROP DESIGN

JOURNAL
Draw your favorite character from the story and share exactly what makes them your favorite

COSTUME DESIGN
Costumes

Boy – hiking shorts, shirt, jacket, boots, backpack, snacks, water bottle, flashlight

Girl – hiking shorts, shirt, jacket, boots, backpack, snacks, water bottle

Mother – camping clothes, t-shirt, plaid shirt, hiking pants, boots

Father – camping clothes, t-shirt, plaid shirt, hiking pants, boots

Owl – feathers out of paper or plastic (See Pinterest for owl costume)

Ouzel – light grey fabric for body and wings

Indigenous storyteller in Wagon Scene – leather shirt/pants with fringe, headband, feather

Settlers in Wagon Scene – jeans, plaid shirts, vests, bandanas, hats, long dresses, bonnets, fire pit

Narrator prospector – old jeans, old plaid shirt, hat, bandana, boots, beard

STAGE PROP CONSTRUCTION
Make a large rainbow

Make a large storybook with an easel

Christmas trees w/o lights

Find one or two small bright colored tents

Construction of Magic Mountain (option is to paint the cardboard mountain)

WEEK 6 PLANNING NOTES

- ❏ Camera or iPhone
- ❏ Journals
- ❏ Pen or pencils
- ❏ Costume work
- ❏ Final prop construction
- ❏ Sound tech
- ❏ Light tech

WEEK 6
DIORAMAS & EARTHWATCH AREAS COMPLETED

DIORAMAS
Complete dioramas

ENVIRONMENT EXPERIMENT
Chart changes in Earthwatch areas
Take pictures
Draw and/or write about the changes in your journal

COSTUMES
Continue working on costumes

STAGE PROPS
Continue working on props

STAGE LIGHTING
Create lighting effects for the night scene and when Magic awakens
Write out lighting needs for tech person

SOUND TECH
Set locations for microphones, if using the stage
Confirm 7 body mics with the music director for narrator or narrators,
    boy, girl, Mom, Dad, owl, Magic

WEEK 7 PLANNING NOTES

❏ Giant layout for storybook

❏ Marker

❏ Create an easel

WEEK 7
COMPLETE CONSTRUCTION - COMPLETE COSTUMES - COMPLETE PROPS

SET CONSTRUCTION
   Begin construction of sets
   Large layout paper storybook for the narrator
   Set staging for the play
   Block stage
   Set cues for each group and actor

COSTUMES
   All animal masks completed
   All costumes completed
   All props completed

PROPS
   Complete props

WEEK 8 PLANNING NOTES

❏ Programs with names for characters and song credits
❏ Giant storybook
❏ Easel
❏ Rocking chair
❏ Lamp
❏ Costumes
❏ Backpacks (2)
❏ Flashlights
❏ Masks
❏ Firepit
❏ Tents
❏ Flowers in pots
❏ Trees
❏ Mountain mural
❏ Sky with clouds
❏ Journals on display (optional)
❏ Dioramas on display (optional)

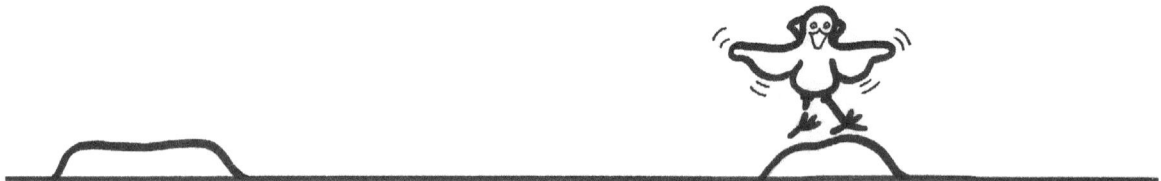

Congratulations! You made it!

WEEK 8
PERFORMANCE & VIDEO

PERFORMANCE OF MAGIC MOUNTAIN THE MUSICAL
❏ Dress rehearsal for friends & family
❏ Programs
❏ The story read by the narrator or prospector
❏ Giant book on easel (optional)
❏ Songs ready to perform
❏ Drums and rattles completed for performance
❏ Journals on display for parents and audience to view (optional)
❏ Dioramas on display (optional)
❏ Staging in place
❏ Video cameras in 2 or 3 angles

VIDEO TECH
Video performance for parents and to archive project
Post on Facebook or YouTube

LIGHT TECH
Someone in place to cue house lights down and up

STAGE MANAGER
The person who coordinates when groups, classes, or actors go on stage

POST PRODUCTION

FEEDBACK AND SHARING
> How did it go? What worked?
> What needed improvement?
> It is always beneficial to check in with students and staff to review what
> worked with this curriculum and what could have gone smoother.

> We welcome all comments and inspirations.

> Please contact me at: lisadancinglight.com

> You did it! Well done. I hope you feel fully satisfied with this whole magical process.
> Thank you for your commitment to bringing the Magic Mountain Art Curriculum
> into your classroom and/or into your family education program.

Lisa Dancing-Light

MAGIC MOUNTAIN®

An Environmental Children's Program

MUSIC CURRICULUM GUIDE

Ages: 4 – 11
Grades: Pre – K through 5th

Lisa Dancing-Light, BME, Educational Specialist

MUSIC CURRICULUM GUIDE

WEEK 1
LISTEN – DRUM – SING

WEEK 2
SING – JOURNAL – ACT

WEEK 3
MOVEMENT – RATTLES – SING

WEEK 4
DRUM – SING – IMAGINE

WEEK 5
MOVE – SING – JOURNAL

WEEK 6
MUSICAL REVIEW

WEEK 7
FINAL REHEARSAL – SETS – PROPS – COSTUMES

WEEK 8
DRESS REHEARSAL – PERFORMANCE & VIDEO

POST PRODUCTION

WEEK 1
LISTEN – DRUM – SING

    Brain Gym

    Talking Circle

    Name Game/Rhythm Instruments

    Qigong movemet

    Sing Sacred Ground

    Read Magic Mountain

    Sing Magic Mountain chorus and 1st verse

    Journals

WEEK 2
SING – JOURNAL – ACT

    Brain Gym

    Review Sacred Ground

    Introduce rattles

    Introduce Power Chant

    Review Magic Mountain

    Activity – Use felt or magnet board to act out a story

    Journals – Drawing

    Drama – The children can create a play

WEEK 3
MOVEMENT – RATTLES – SING

    Review Brain Gym

    Review Power Chant with movement

    Review Sacred Ground with rattles and Circle Dance

    Introduce Into the Mountains – 1st verse

    Review Magic Mountain Song – Chorus and 1st and 2nd Verse

WEEK 4
DRUM – SING – IMAGINE

    Review Magic Mountain Story with added songs

    Review Sacred Ground and Power Chant

    Introduce drums or make drums

    Introduce Coyote Singing

    Magic Mountain – Introduce 3rd verse

    Introduce Into the Mountains 2nd verse

    Introduce Winnebago Song 1st verse

    Introduce The Ouzel Song

Introduce Postcard Chorus
Children can plan and take a pretend trip - Musical Chairs Game

WEEK 5
MOVE – SING – JOURNAL
    Movement & Rhythm – Ice skating with paper plates
    Review songs
        Sacred Ground – Introduce sign language
        Power Chant
        Coyote Singing
        The Winnebago Song 2nd verse
        The Ouzel Song – Introduce dance
        Into the Mountains – Introduce 3rd verse
        Magic Mountain – All verses
    Introduce Reduce, Reuse, and Recycle
    Optional – Introduce flute and read a story about the flute
    Magic Mountain journal time

WEEK 6
MUSICAL REVIEW
    Review all songs
    Act out different groups

WEEK 7
FINAL REHEARSAL – SETS – PROPS – COSTUMES
    Review all songs and parts
    Set construction
    Props
    Costumes
    Stage bow

WEEK 8
DRESS REHEARSAL – PERFORMANCE AND VIDEO
    Performance celebration
    Film or video

POST PRODUCTION

WEEK 1
PLANNING NOTES

- ❏ Brain Gym exercises
- ❏ Qigong – Swinging and drumming
- ❏ Talking Stick
- ❏ Rhythm instruments
- ❏ A Song and Story of Magic Mountain
- ❏ Sacred Ground CD and/or sheet music
- ❏ Magic Mountain music CD and/or sheet music
- ❏ Magic Mountain journals
- ❏ Pencil or pen

WEEK 1
LISTEN – DRUM – SING

1. Brain Gym (Watch lisadancinglight.com/tutorial)
   a. Thinking Caps
   b. Brain Buttons

2. Talking Circle
   a. Introduce the Talking Stick, sitting in a circle
   b. Each child has a turn saying their name and passing the Talking Stick

3. Name Game/Rhythm Instruments – Voice, hand drum, the body
   a. Each child can say their name again rhythmically
      i. Example: Ma-son or Ly-di-a
   b. Each child then says their name while clapping the rhythm
   c. Introduce the drum and talk about rhythm and heartbeat
   d. Circle then practices drumbeat on their legs
   e. Pass the drum around the circle for each child to drum their name

4. Qigong movement
   a. Children stand an arm's length apart for Swinging and Drumming
      Watch lisadancinglight.com/tutorial

5. Introduce Sacred Ground
   a. Listen to Magic Mountain Songs CD or YouTube Sacred Ground -
      POINT OF BALANCE - Lisa Dancing-Light
   b. Sing Sacred Ground four times
   c. What does "sacred" mean to them?
   d. How is the Earth sacred?
   e. Teach the Sacred Ground Circle Dance: Step 1: Join hands or place hands on
      hips, moving CLOCKWISE lead with LEFT foot, repeat, practice
      movement. Step 2: Add song, and Step 3: Add rattles

6. Read A SONG AND STORY OF MAGIC MOUNTAIN
   a. Introduce and play the song MAGIC MOUNTAIN
      Go to the website and CLICK on the arrow: lisadancinglight.com
   b. Teach the chorus "Tell Me Magic Mountain" and 1st verse

7. Have children write in their journals about what they remember about the story
   Have them draw a picture of Magic Mountain

WEEK 2

PLANNING NOTES

- ❏ Rattles
- ❏ Magic Mountain book
- ❏ Felt board or magnetic board with felt animals for storytelling
- ❏ Magic Mountain journals
- ❏ Pens and/or pencils
- ❏ Costumes
- ❏ Animal masks (confirm completion with Art Teacher)

WEEK 2
SING – JOURNAL – ACT

Brain Gym
Cross Crawl
The Owl

Sing - Review Sacred Ground
Rhythm
Introduce the rattle
Discuss what is special about the rattle as it is passed around the circle
Discuss the different sounds with rice, beans, corn, rocks, and sand
Hand out rattles and sing Sacred Ground while using them

Power Chant
Listen to Magic Mountain Songs CD or YouTube Power Chant
Sing with children singing the echo and discuss what an echo is
Discuss what power is and where we get our power
Discuss our heartbeat and demonstrate drumming, keeping the beat
Have a child play the drum

Review MAGIC MOUNTAIN story
Retell the story, if necessary, if some children were absent
Ask the children to remember one of the song verses
Sing the song and have the children sing the chorus
Can the children share what stories Magic might tell them?
Can the children share what clothes the boy and girl should wear when hiking?
What clothes might the early settlers have worn?

Activity
Use felt or a magnetic board to talk about the animals living on Magic Mountain

Journals
Drawing

Drama
Have the children dress up in costumes with animal masks

WEEK 3
PLANNING NOTES
- ❏ Power Chant with movement
- ❏ Sacred Ground with rattles
- ❏ Into the Mountains Verse 1
- ❏ Magic Mountain chorus, Verses 1 & 2

WEEK 3
MOVEMENT – RATTLES – SING

Review Brain Gym

Review songs
>Power Chant – Add arm movements
>Sacred Ground – Do circle dance

Introduce Into the Mountains
>Listen to Magic Mountain Songs CD or YouTube Lisa Dancing-Light
>Learn 1st verse

Review Magic Mountain chorus, Verse 1 & 2

WEEK 4
PLANNING NOTES

❏ Sacred Ground

❏ Power Chant

❏ Drums

❏ Coyote Singing

❏ Magic Mountain Verse 3

❏ Into the Mountains Verse 2

❏ The Winnebago Song Verse 1

❏ The Ouzel Song

❏ Postcard

❏ Chairs

WEEK 4
DRUM – SING – IMAGINE

Review Magic Mountain story with some songs added

Review Sacred Ground with circle dance and/or rattles

Review Power Chant with drumming or arm movements

Introduce drums (if available) or make drums

Introduce Coyote Singing
   Listen to Magic Mountain Songs CD or YouTube Lisa Dancing-Light
   Talk about what Coyote would sing to and celebrate.

Magic Mountain - Introduce 3rd verse

Introduce Into the Mountains 2nd verse

Introduce The Winnebago Song
   Listen to Magic Mountain Songs CD or YouTube Lisa Dancing-Light
      Introduce Winnebago chorus

Introduce The Ouzel Song
   Listen to Magic Mountain Songs CD or YouTube Lisa Dancing-Light
   Discuss the American Dipper or Water Ouzel
   Show picture

Introduce Postcard chorus
   Listen to Magic Mountain Songs CD or YouTube Lisa Dancing-Light
   Audition duet singers
   Give singers music scores and recordings

Theater
   The children can take a pretend trip with chairs set up like a bus or car
   They can discuss what they would take on their trip
   They can discuss where they would want to go and how they would get there

WEEK 5
PLANNING NOTES

- ❏ Paper plates
- ❏ Sacred Ground
- ❏ Power Chant
- ❏ Coyote Singing
- ❏ The Ouzel Song – Ouzel Dance
- ❏ The Winnebago Song Verse 2
- ❏ Into the Mountains Verse 3
- ❏ Magic Mountain Chorus and all 3 verses
- ❏ Flute
- ❏ Flute story
- ❏ Reduce, Reuse, Recycle song
- ❏ Magic Mountain journal

The Ouzel Dance

Variation One: One child plays the Ouzel dipping up and down with bent legs, hands on waist, elbow bent moving forward and backward.

Variation Two: 3 – 6 dancers play Ouzels doing same movement as above.

Blocking steps:

Step left, together (7 times) Say: *"Step-together, step-together," etc.*

8th time - step back on left foot, pivot halfway facing back, pull right foot in

Step left, together (7 steps) 8th step same as above

Repeat #1 and #2

4 steps forward – right-left, right-left, right-left, right-left

4 steps back - right-left, right-left, right-left, right-left

Repeat #5 and #6

Just like a child, you **bend** your knees, **Dancing** to the rhythm of the **flowing** water
Step left-together,   left-together,   left-together,   left-together,
Stepping so close to the **edge** of the riverbed, **Take** a step back and **turn** around.
Left-together,   left-together,   left-together,   left foot back turn around
Ouzel dance, **Ouzel** sing with me, **Ouzel** dipping by the **river's** edge
Left-together, left-together,   left-together,   left-together,
Ouzel dance, **Ouzel** sing with me, **Celebrate** your kinship with the **family** of life.
Left-together, left-together,   left-together,   left foot back turn around

               La-la-la-la, **La**-la-la-la-la-la
Forward **Right**-*left, right-left, right-left, right-left*
               La-la-la-la. **La**-la-la-la *repeat*
Back   **Right**-*left, right-left, right-left, right-left repeat*

48

WEEK 5
MOVE – SING – JOURNAL

Movement and rhythm
  Introduce ice skating by placing paper plates on the floor under each foot.
    Practice slow, smooth movements to music

Introduce Ouzel Dance
  (see previous page for instructions)

Review songs
  Sacred Ground – Introduce sign language
  Power Chant
  Coyote Singing
  The Winnebago Song
  The Ouzel Song
  Into the Mountains
  Magic Mountain

Introduce Reduce, Reuse & Recycle
  Listen to Magic Mountain Songs CD or YouTube Lisa Dancing-Light

Flute
  Introduce the flute and read a story about the Native American flute
    (for example: *The Courting Flute Native American Tradition* by Ed Wapp, Jr.)

Art and journal time
  Draw in Magic Mountain journals

WEEK 6

PLANNING NOTES

Review

❏ Sacred Ground

❏ Power Chant

❏ Coyote Singing

❏ The Ouzel Song

❏ Into the Mountains

❏ Postcard

❏ Magic Mountain

❏ Reduce, Reuse & Recycle

❏ The Winnebago Song – Verse 3

WEEK 6
MUSICAL REVIEW

Review
    Sacred Ground
    Circle dance
    Rattles
    Power Chant
    Arm movements
    Drumming

Review

Power Chant	1:57
Sacred Ground	1:03
Postcard	4:24
The Ouzel Song	1:34
The Winnebago Song	2:07
Into the Mountains	3:15
Coyote Singing	1:44
Reduce, Reuse & Recycle	1:26
Magic Mountain	3:22

Additional songs for longer play

Starwalker (Point of Balance)	4:27
Trilogy (Point of Balance)	7:18
The Mother Earth Chant	
The Reply	
The Promise	
Point of Balance (Point of Balance)	6:07
Children of the Earth (Point of Balance)	3:31

Magic Mountain
    Rehearse different groups for the forest, animals, drummers, rattle people, and listeners

WEEK 7
PLANNING NOTES
Review
- ❏ Power Chant
- ❏ Sacred Ground
- ❏ Postcard
- ❏ The Ouzel Song
- ❏ The Winnebago Song
- ❏ Into the Mountains
- ❏ Coyote Singing
- ❏ Reduce, Reuse & Recycle
- ❏ Magic Mountain

Props
- ❏ Rattles in basket
- ❏ Costumes

WEEK 7
FINAL REHEARSAL – SETS – PROPS – COSTUMES

Review all songs
    Power Chant
    Sacred Ground
    Postcard
    The Ouzel Song
    The Winnebago Song - Chorus
    Into the Mountains
    Coyote Singing
    Reduce, Reuse & Recycle
    Magic Mountain

Magic Mountain
    Read *A Song and Story of Magic Mountain* with songs included
    Add staging and scenes for each song
    Add stories that groups have created.
    Add masks and rhythm instruments into the story

Set construction
Props
Costumes
    (Consult Art Teacher and other instructors to see what needs to be completed

Rehearse the stage bow

WEEK 8
PLANNING NOTES

Props
- ❏ Rattles in basket
- ❏ Flashlights
- ❏ Tents
- ❏ Backpacks
- ❏ Masks
- ❏ Costumes
- ❏ Storybook
- ❏ Easel
- ❏ Rocking chair
- ❏ Lamp

WEEK 8
DRESS REHEARSAL – PERFORMANCE AND VIDEO

Magic Mountain
  Read the story with songs and instruments
  Rehearse with costumes and staging with scenes and lighting

Review Songs
  Power Chant – Small group song or entrance song with all singing
  Sacred Ground – Young group
  Postcard – Girl and/or boy solo
  The Ouzel Song – Small group song and dance
  The Winnebago Song – Mother and Father sing with a group chorus
  Into the Mountains – All sing
  Coyote Singing – Small group song with drumming
  Reduce, Reuse & Recycle – Magic sings, and all sing chorus
  Magic Mountain – All sing

Video cameras set up
Lighting tech set
Stage manager set for entrance cues
Programs on the table or handed out by a student

ALTERNATIVE SONGS
  Go to YouTube Lisa Dancing-Light
      Point of Balance 6:05 Solo and group
      The Trilogy 7:18 Solo indigenous character
      Starwalker 4:30 Girl and/or boy solo
      Children of the Earth 3:30 Solo

POST PRODUCTION

FEEDBACK AND SHARING

It is always beneficial to check in with students and staff to review what worked well with this curriculum and what could have been added or gone smoother.

We welcome all comments and inspirations and would love to hear from you. Please contact us: lisadancinglight.com.

Thank you for your commitment to bringing the Magic Mountain Music Curriculum into your classroom and/or your family educational program.

Lisa Dancing-Light

MAGIC MOUNTAIN®

An Environmental Children's Program

Outdoor Education Guide for Young Explorers

Ages: 4 – 11

Grades: Pre – K through 5th

Lisa Dancing-Light, BME, Educational Specialist

©2021 Dancing Light Enterprises, LLC

OUTDOOR EDUCATION GUIDE
FOR YOUNG EXPLORERS

1. **OUTDOOR DISCOVERY OBJECTIVES**

2. **DAY HIKE FIELD TRIP**

3. **BACKPACKING**

4. **READING AND STORYTELLING**

5. **WEATHER AWARENESS AND FOREST FIRE PREVENTION**

6. **CAMPING TRIP AND PREPARATION**

7. **EARTH SCIENCE AND GEOLOGY**

8. **ENVIRONMENTAL ISSUES LAWS, AND REGULATIONS**

9. **SCIENCE EXPERIMENTS**

10. **PHYSICAL TRAINING**

1. OUTDOOR DISCOVERY OBJECTIVES

A. Mountain Wildlife

    Bird Identification:
- ❏ Discover different birds in your neighborhood
- ❏ Take their pictures and learn their names

    High Alpine Animals Identification:
- ❏ Identification of these animals

B. High Alpine Flora and Vegetation:
- ❏ Learn the names of the flora and vegetation
- ❏ What are some names of high alpine trees?

C. Geology and Minerals:
- ❏ Explore the different geology that makes up mountain terrain
- ❏ What kinds of minerals are found in the mountains?

D. Mountain Weather:
- ❏ How to learn about Mountain Weather Systems

2. DAY HIKE FIELD TRIP

A. Backpacking Preparation:
- ❏ What would you take on a day hike?
- ❏ How would you dress to prepare for the appropriate weather conditions?
- ❏ What kind of shoes would you wear?

B. Map Reading Skills:
- ❏ Can you learn how to use a map and develop directional skills?
- ❏ Do you know how to use a compass?

3. BACKPACKING
- ❏ How would you prepare for a backpacking trip?
- ❏ How would you carry your gear?
- ❏ What would the basics include?
- ❏ How will you get your drinking water?

4. READING AND STORYTELLING

❑ Read a book about camping or hiking in the wilderness
❑ Write a story about your experience or make one up
❑ What is the point of storytelling?
❑ *The Legend of Jumping Mouse* – John Steptoe
❑ Building Vocabulary – Can you list the new words you learned from this Magic Mountain story?

5. WEATHER AWARENESS AND FOREST FIRE PREVENTION

❑ How would you prepare for changing weather?
❑ What is the safest place to be during a storm?
❑ What is hyperthermia?
❑ What causes thunder and lightning?
❑ How do you think global warming affects high alpine climate snowfall?
❑ What are observable signs of vegetation and moisture?
❑ Forest Fire and Prevention – Controlled Burns vs. Natural Growth:
    ❑ Learn about Fire Prevention
    ❑ What is the benefit of controlled burns vs. natural growth?
       See the Earth Science section at Ducksters.com
    ❑ What is the cause of forest fires?
    ❑ Are forest fires good?
    ❑ What is the benefit of controlled burns vs. natural growth?
    ❑ Learn about Fire Prevention

6. CAMPING TRIP AND PREPARATION

A. BASIC FIRST AID
    ❑ What would you do if you got injured?
    ❑ What would you put in a first aid kit?
    ❑ How would you treat someone with an allergic reaction?

B. MOUNTAIN SURVIVAL
    ❑ What steps would you take if you got lost?

C. MAP READING
    ❑ Bring a map to class
    ❑ Locate different places on this map
    ❑ Bring a topographical map to class
    ❑ Discuss how to use this type of map

D. FIRE STARTING
- ❏ Search: Starting a Fire Without Matches
- ❏ Search: Fire Safety and Awareness

E. FOOD
- ❏ Plan and prepare a campfire meal
- ❏ Do you know about food storage in the wilderness to prevent attracting bears?
- ❏ Do you know safe edible plants or how to wildcraft foods?
- ❏ What are some edible high alpine foods?
- ❏ Identify edible sources of food in the wild

F. PERSONAL HYGIENE
- ❏ Do you know how to use a solar shower?
- ❏ What would you do with your personal waste?

G. MATH
- ❏ Meal Planning – Use your math skills to calculate how much food to bring on your trip for you or your class
- ❏ Vary the number of camping days to decide how much food and water to bring
- ❏ How many ounces of water should you drink every day?
- ❏ Research and compare heights of different mountains
- ❏ Use graph paper to illustrate the heights of mountains drawn to scale
- ❏ Decide/guess when the mountain was born and calculate its age today
- ❏ Calculate the number of steps to walk up a mountain, or on a hike

7. EARTH SCIENCE AND GEOLOGY
- ❏ How are mountains formed?
- ❏ What are tectonic plates?
- ❏ Explore the different geology that makes up mountain terrain
- ❏ Research and compare heights of different mountains
- ❏ Use graph paper to illustrate heights of mountains drawn to scale
- ❏ What is the difference between a mineral and a rock?
- ❏ What kinds of minerals are found in the mountains?
- ❏ What are properties of minerals?
- ❏ Is there mining in the area?
- ❏ What kinds of mines can be in the mountains? Coal, marble, gold, silver
- ❏ What are the benefits and hazards of mining
- ❏ Do you know why there are laws to prevent pollution from the extraction process?
- ❏ What is the impact on rivers, wildlife, traffic

❏ Visit a mining reclamation projects in your area
❏ Was it successful or did it fail?
❏ Resource: Earth Science for Kids www.Ducksters.com

8. ENVIRONMENTAL ISSUES, LAWS, AND REGULATIONS

❏ Research Laws and Regulations
❏ How do they impact in the area where you are hiking?
❏ Government Policies
❏ What are some of the government policies?
❏ Logging and Road Development
❏ What laws govern logging and road development in National Forests?
❏ Mining
❏ What are some issues with mining in your area?
  See Ducksters.com Earth Science

9. SCIENCE EXPERIMENTS

❏ Search cool science experiments for kids
❏ Air pollution experiment
❏ Search make your own compost
❏ Search how to make compost in a bottle
❏ Search create a water filter

10. PHYSICAL TRAINING

❏ What types of exercises would you do to create a Training Program for a hiking or backpacking expedition?
❏ Imagine you are hiking on a tall mountain and how you would exercise to prepare for it.

REVIEW AND ASSESSMENT

It is always beneficial to check in with students and staff to review what worked with this Outdoor Explorer Curriculum and what could have been more appropriate, more fun, and more beneficial.

Would you like to share your photos and experiences?

Visit Facebook MagicMountainBook or lisadancinglight.com.

Thank you for your commitment to bringing Magic Mountain Outdoor Curriculum for Young Explorers into your classroom and/or into your family educational program.

Lisa Dancing-Light

To order additional Magic Mountain materials please visit:

lisadancinglight.com

- A Song and Story of Magic Mountain – English and Spanish translation
- Magic Mountain – The Musical
- Magic Mountain Puzzles
- Magic Mountain Songs CD
- Magic Mountain Activity/Coloring Book

ACKNOWLEDGMENTS

A program of this magnitude would not be possible without my own journey and adventures along with years of research, exploration, and deep contemplation. The process of assembling these ideas involved decades of magical inspiration and creative mining. The initial song entitled Magic Mountain was composed in 1981 when my sons were in preschool. The initial concept for the story of Magic Mountain was based on the song and conceived when I was invited to write an environmental music event and curriculum for the Colorado Rocky Mountain School (CRMS Preschool) where I was teaching piano and voice.

Those whose names I can recall were part of the beginning journey of Magic Mountain and deserve my deepest gratitude and appreciation. Debbie Condello, director of Colorado Rocky Mountain School (CRMS Preschool), was the great inspiration and supporter of the project, and teachers Jeannie Clark and Molly Child provided invaluable classroom and rehearsal support. There were many students and faculty who stood by to help with the staging and production at CRMS. Mary Noone, a Glenwood Springs artist, constructed the life-size talking mountain out of canvas. Channel 4 from Denver provided the archival footage which I still treasure in VCR format. CRMS Preschool also received a grant from Carbondale Council on the Arts and Humanities.

Forty years later, Magic Mountain was revived as I read the story to my granddaughter's Montessori preschool in Salt Lake City, seeing that the theme was still poignant and carried a message that inspired children.

When the director said that she could write a whole semester curriculum based on this little story, a seed was planted which has blossomed into the curriculum guide that you are now reading.

I am so grateful for the opportunity to test drive this curriculum and to be the musical director for my first original MAGIC MOUNTAIN® musical at Marble Charter School in Marble, Colorado.

I wish to thank Grace M. Zanni for laying out the original Curriculum Guidelines that charted the course for this adventure.

The most unique part of this whole process is trying to communicate what is in my imagination and translate that to physical reality. For that, I owe a debt of gratitude to Alyssa Ohnmacht at Light of the Moon, Inc. who spent countless hours with me as we navigated our way through page after page of creative content.

May this program be fun, motivational, and rewarding.

May it bring great joy and wonder and may it enrich your life.

Lisa Dancing-Light

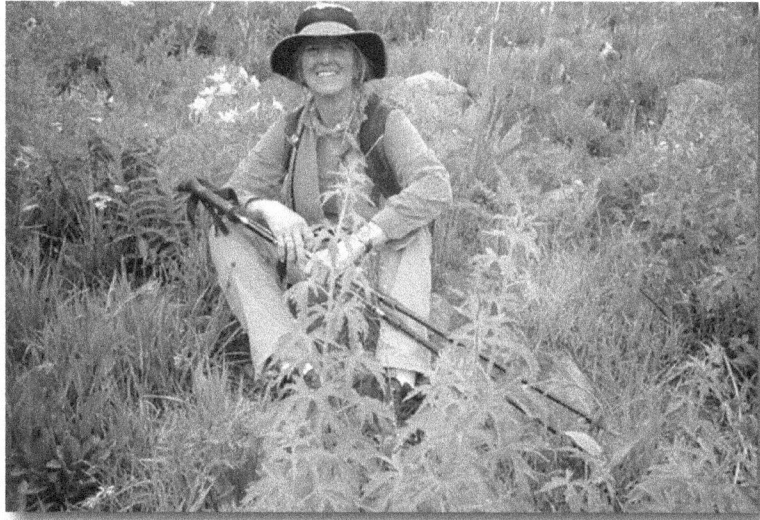

Lisa Dancing-Light • Author

Lisa Dancing-Light is an internationally recognized recording artist and composer, a teller of stories, a singer of songs, and a tender of gardens. With a degree in Music Education, Lisa has been an educational specialist for forty years and is certified in the Suzuki Piano Method.

She first fell in love with the magic and mystery of nature as a child hunting for strawberries in her mother's garden. This love of nature was further nurtured by horseback riding in Colorado and later traveling and hiking in Alaska, Australia, New Zealand, Peru, Ireland, Italy, and France.

Lisa is the former Director of Music at Aspen Community School and has taught at Colorado Rocky Mountain School and Ross Montessori School. She also helped score five musicals performed at the Wheeler Opera House in Aspen. Her musical garden has produced five globally-streamed recordings of original compositions.

As a master gardener, she loves sharing wisdom of the natural world with her grandchildren. She also enjoys watching bees, deer, ducks, and geese while hunting strawberries and picking pumpkins in her garden.

Lisa currently lives in Colorado and has journeyed many times to the top of Mount Sopris, the inspiration for Magic Mountain.